Loss

LOSS

DONNA ASHWORTH

BLACK & WHITE PUBLISHING

First published in the UK in 2022 by
Black & White Publishing Ltd
Nautical House, 104 Commercial Street, Edinburgh, EH6 6NF

A division of Bonnier Books UK
4th Floor, Victoria House, Bloomsbury Square, London, WC1B 4DA
Owned by Bonnier Books
Sveavägen 56, Stockholm, Sweden

A CIP catalogue record for this book is available from the British Library.

ISBN: 978 1 78530 442 2

7 9 10 8 6

Typeset by Iolaire Typesetting, Newtonmore
Printed and bound in Great Britain by Clays Ltd, Elcograf S.p.A.

www.blackandwhitepublishing.com

I dedicate this book to all those who have shared their grief with me over the last few years, so that I may better understand the nature of its wrath and the many complicated faces it wears. Your insight, your undying love, your connection, has brought me here.

AUTHOR'S NOTE

This book is for those lost on that violent sea of grief, or washed up on a lonely island waiting to feel alive enough again to return to the mainland. This book is not a cure, for there is no such thing. Rather it is a mirror to reflect your suffering back, but this time with comfort and perhaps a little more clarity. This book is a reminder that you are not alone, that this heartbreak connects each and every human alike.

In short, this book is a place to dwell when no other place fits. You can grieve here, my friend. It is very much okay to grieve here.

CONTENTS

what is grief

if not just love

turned inside out

and upside down

HOW TO TALK TO THE GRIEVING

Do not fear
how you will speak
to the grieving
providing you never say
it's time to move on

for that is not possible.

They are in a world of pain
and whilst you cannot help them
your kindness has weight.

So just show up
or stay away
depending on their pain level
that day.

But show you care.

And be very sure to remind them
that the person they are missing *mattered*.

You cannot choose the wrong words
if you let your soul do the talking
to their soul.

And if you listen closely
the person who has left
may help you
with your quest to comfort.

Or perhaps they will urge you
to simply wrap their loved one
in your arms.

WHERE YOU LEFT ME

Don't expect me to be where you left me
I can't promise to wait for you there
I may not see the flowers you gave me
or the tears that will fall as you stare

I will be with the winds on the coastlines
embracing the mountains of snow
I'll be dancing around on the hillsides
lighting the fires that glow

I'll be flying with geese for the winter
and welcoming lambs as they're born
I'll be singing with choirs in the theatre
free roaming without any form

Don't expect me to lie where you laid me
there is so much that I wish to do
but I promise with all of my heart
that the first place I'll visit is you.

LET ME GO

When I'm gone
don't fret over the things I left behind
you don't need those trinkets
to remember what we had.

And if you fear the forgetting
I will remind you when you sleep
and you will wake up smiling

don't let that turn to tears
for I meant to bring joy.

When I'm gone
don't fuss over my house
or my clothes
or my organs
give them all away
for they mean nothing
where I am
and someone who has time left
could use them
very much.

When I'm gone
fight that sadness
and only let it fly its flag
on days when you most need to.

My birthday
should be celebrated still
for I was alive and I *lived*
and that must be remembered
above all.

When I'm gone
let me go my love
and say my name often
for I think that will be the sign I need
to come from wherever I may be.

But when I do
don't say you miss me
because that I already know

just say you love me
and that you let me go

you have to let me go.

A DREAM

When they told me you were gone
when they said you'd passed away
there was nothing in my lungs
but
empty
space

The ground beneath me swam
blood was rushing in my ears
and my newly broken heart
began
to
race

When they uttered those sharp words
when they tried to hold me close
I felt that no one else could
hear
me
scream

When they told me you were gone
that you never would return
how I wished that this was only
just
a
dream.

WIDER THAN THE WORLD

There's a space
where you once sat my love
wider than the world itself

bigger than the point of all life.

I tiptoe
small steps
around that space.

I live a full day fearing it
knowing the pain it holds within.

Sometimes I feel a surge of courage
and rush towards it
ready to dive
be consumed
by the past
by the memories
by the pain
by *you*.

What sweet hell that would be.

One day I will go inside it
and meet you there
just for a moment
when time weaves me a cloak
to protect from the burn
and your love becomes the cushion
that bears the brunt of the impact.

For now
I tiptoe around the space

that's wider than the world itself.

THE LOST HALF

Ah but what is left
when half of you is gone?

How does that half
learn how to carry on?

How does that half
face the world alone?

How does that half
let go of all it's known?

How does that half
rise up from bed each day?

Knowing that its partner
won't be there
to show the way?

A half without its half
needs to learn to breathe again.

Forever thinking of its half
its soulmate
and best friend.

INSIDE OUT

Get used to grief my friend
for once it calls
it does not take its leave

*an unwanted guest
but a guest nonetheless
and a guest
we must receive.*

Get used to grief my friend
for once it's with you
it sticks like sea to shore

*the folks who grieve
get no reprieve
just the learning
to live once more.*

Get used to grief my friend
for when it arrives
it won't be escorted out

*so usher it in
let the grief win
it's love
turned inside out.*

IT'S YOUR BIRTHDAY TODAY

It's your birthday today
and the same
as every year

I vow to fight the dark
I try to keep
you near

I try to play your music
and make the cake
you like

I try to say your name
and pretend the world's
alright

I count the years without you
shocked at how
they've flown

I think about the children
and how you'd think
they've grown

It's your birthday today
and the same as
every year

I try to see your face
through the veil of
lost love's tears.

RAINBOW BRIDGE

There's a place in the sky
where the animals live
it's a wonderful place indeed
there's no malice
no envy
no hate in their hearts
just creatures
of every creed.

It's the place they ascend to
when time has run out
full of wide open spaces to run
there's unlimited food
no shortage of toys
and the aim
of the day
is just fun.

And while there's no question
this place is divine
there's a hole in your world
this I know
but think of your baby
so happy
so free
be kind enough to
let them go.

SORRY FOR YOUR LOSS

When I say *sorry for your loss*
it may sound perfunctory
trite even

but what I mean is

I am sorry
that you wake in the night
gasping for breath
heart racing in agony.

I am sorry
that you will know a lifetime
of *what ifs* and
could have beens.

I am sorry
that you ache
for one more minute with your love
knowing it can never be.

When I say *sorry for your loss*
please know
my soul is reaching out to yours
in understanding
and trying very hard
to take away
just one little ounce of your pain.

THE GHOSTS

You have always been surrounded
when you needed it most
by ghosts.

Those who left you in this life
those who went before you
and those who went before them.

Generations of ghosts
connected by love
like a silvery thread
that's stitched between you all.

Each one appearing
when their guidance is required
each one a different light
a different feeling
a different way
but always love.

But fear not
it is only the ghosts
who are connected by love
which visit you still.

There is a great reason for that

love is the thread
love is the thread.

THE LOSS OF A MOTHER

is an inevitable part of our life.

We know it will come around
and we know the day will hurt
but we are not prepared
never prepared
for the *tearing*.

The tearing of a part of our soul
from its very seams
stitches pulled asunder
heart wrenched in half
soul split in two.

But that tearing is not what you may think
it is not her leaving you
it is the loss of her physical form
which you have been
so very used and attached to.

And now she must remove that part
for it no longer serves you
and you no longer need it
despite what you may think.

Because she made you well
and she built all of her love into you

cell by cell
thought by thought
lesson by lesson.

And the split that you feel
is simply the new way
you will carry on your love
for your mother

with your mother
just in a different way

*for she did not leave
mothers cannot leave*

they are in you
look inside
she's there
and that is unable to be taken now
that is all yours to keep

forevermore.

THE LOSS OF A FATHER

is the anchor pulled from the seabed
the steering wheel unhinged
the mast split by lighting
and the bow broken by storm.

The ship you sail
now feels unsafe
no longer weatherproof
without direction
or brave heart
to speed its way.

Perhaps you did not even know
that he was your compass
that you gazed upon his lead
like a north-star in the night.

He gave you all of this
you see
without notice or congratulation
diligently
consistently
continuously guiding
always showing the way
in the way he knew how.

And whilst you are cast adrift
I know this to be true
you will anchor yourself once more
when you realise
that his voice still speaks
still guides
still brings a brave heart your way
in the roughest of storms.

And the answers you seek
he already planted deep
for he knew one day

you would need to sail alone.

So he buried little pieces of himself
within your heart
your mind
your spirit
and your soul

little breadcrumbs of love
to show the way

home.

GREAT GRIEF

Don't fall out of love with the world
because they no longer live in it.

Instead be grateful
that this world *produced* them

be glad
that this life ever existed

and that *you*
were blessed enough
to love them then

and love them still.

Don't fall out of love with this world
because it could not keep
your heart whole

instead

let love be the glue
patch it up
and fill it with joy
joy that you know
first-hand
in this bittersweet conundrum

that great grief
is born only
of great love.

THE BOX

I keep the things
I didn't say to you
in a box
inside my heart.

And one day
when I am strong
or foolish enough
I will open it.

And in that box
there will be a note that says
*tell everyone how you feel
every day.*

Because I didn't tell you enough
that I loved you
every minute
every second
of every day.

So now I keep those words
for you
in that box
I keep them as a reminder
not to add
any more
never to add
any more.

ONCE A DAY

Don't miss me more than once a day
for life is moving fast
don't wish all of your time away
dreaming of the past

Don't waste the moment looking at
the things I left behind me
I'm not there anymore my love
your heart is where you'll find me

Don't dread to say my name sweet one
don't fear the wrath of sadness
just take the love you had for me
and turn it into gladness

Some days your anger will rush out
your tears will find their way
to me, wherever I am then
I'll soothe them all away

When I am gone don't miss me more
than once or twice a day
there's so much life to live my love
I'm with you all the way.

SOME DAYS ARE FOR THE GRIEF

Some days are just for grief
no joy
no memories
no reminiscing fondly
of all that was shared

just soul-sucking
heart wrenching
grief.

Some days are for the grief
and that's okay.

But on the days
when grief is love again
when the weight of loss
lifts a little
let that love out
let that love shine forth
like the beacon of hope that it is.

Some days are for the love
and that's okay.

This journey is a balancing act.

Just balance.

I LET GO OF YOUR HAND

I don't recall
the day I stopped holding your hand
was I ten
maybe younger
I wonder if you noticed
that I had let go for the final time?

I held your hand again
so many many years later
at the end
and that bittersweet image
will stay with me forevermore.

And I long for all the days in between
when your hand stayed without mine.

Days where I did not wrap your hand
with love
inside my own
and I wonder why not?

I would give anything I own
to hold that hand one more time.

And when I get the chance again
I will not let go so easily.

SOMETIMES

Sometimes a bullet
sometimes a kiss
my grief takes aim
and does not miss

Sometimes the truth
sometimes a lie
my dreams
the only alibi

Sometimes a rumble
sometimes a roar
the loss I feel
growls evermore

Sometimes thunder
sometimes rain
always there
yet never the same.

TAKE THE LOVE

Take the love you had for me
and turn it into laughter
turn it into blinding light
to shine on you thereafter

Take the love you have for me
and show it to the world
something so amazing
needs to blossom and unfurl

Take the love that made us
keep it burning bright
let that fire guide you
let it warm you through the night

Take the love you shared with me
and spread it out with gladness
my life will not have been in vain
if you can fight the sadness

Take the love my darling
it's yours to carry on
grow that love forevermore
and then I won't be gone.

AGAINST THE GRAIN

A grief that goes against
the generational grain
is the toughest of all to take
because it is not the natural order of life.

There is no comfort to be found
in the having lived a life
there is no *as it should be*
no why
no reason
no salve.

There are only a million
missed moments
a billion *why them*
and a trillion
I would take their place in a heartbeat.

A grief that goes against
the generational grain
is the toughest of all to take
because it's wrong

it's just all so very wrong.

DEATH IS A THIEF

Death is a thief that hides out of sight
and waits for the living to age
it pulls at the breath and claws at the heart
it thrives on the grief and the rage

Death is a cloud that swallows the sky
and puts out the light of the moon
it knows not of love or the ache of a loss
it cares not for years gone too soon

Death is a cancer that eats at the soul
and feasts on the salt in our tears
it rides with the darkness on waves of sheer pain
and thrives on the depth of our fears

Death is a beast and that can't be unsaid
but there's one thing that beast cannot find
the love in my heart is locked tight with a key
it will always, forever, be mine.

HOLIDAY GRIEF

The festive season
'the most wonderful time of the year'
but if you are missing a face at your table
it can be the hardest time of all.

How to feel merry
how to feel bright
when your world
has lost its light?

How to carry on
continue the traditions
when the person who made it all worthwhile
is not there?

How to face the music
the dancing
the cheering
and the reflection of a year gone by
when the pain is already suffocating
on an ordinary day?

You just try.

It is all you can do my friend.

You try, very hard
to imagine
what that person would tell you
and if you listen really closely
you will hear it
in their voice.

What would they want you to do?
Retreat?
Isolate?
Or take their favourite songs
and their funny stories
and their little festive habits
and share it with your loves?

In their honour
now that they cannot

I think we can all agree
it is what they would wish for you
I think we can also agree
that they would want you
to feel as loved
as you once did when they were here.

They would want you to feel their love *still*.

They are trying very hard to make you feel it.

It hasn't gone away.

And you need that love now
more than ever
and everyone around you
needs it too.

So, feel their love, say their name
bring them back to your festive table
even if it takes all of your courage and heart.

It is the only *way*.

SWEET CHILD

When a light is as bright
as the light you shone
there's no such thing
as truly gone

When a smile is as precious
as the one you wore
you nestle in hearts
forevermore

When one so loved
is taken too soon
the love that is left
could outshine the moon

So much love with no place
to be truly at peace
so we love you more
bittersweet release

Sweet child
you were here
for so little in time
but the hole that you left

grows ever wide.

WHEN I GO

When I go
don't learn to live without me
just learn to live with my love
in a different way.

And if you need to see me
close your eyes
or look in your shadow
when the sun shines

I'm there.

Sit with me in the quiet
and you will know
that I did not leave.

There is no leaving
when one soul is blended
with another.

When I go
don't learn to live without me
just learn to look for me
in the moments.

I will *be there*.

THE LAST TIME

I think I held your hand
the last time
I know I had to haste away
I should have been content to stay
that thought haunts me daily
the last time

I should have said so many things
the last time
I should have reminisced some more
brought wondrous memories
to your door
I could have said *I love you*
the last time

I hope you felt my unsaid words
the last time
I hope the things I didn't say
found your heart anyway
that's all that I can hope for
the last time

I sometimes wish for one more
last time
I sometimes lie awake at night
to hear your voice with all my might
if only I had listened more
the last time

There is one very troubling thing
with *last times*
they don't announce when they are here
they do not warn you
there's no fear
so treat each living minute
as a *last time*.

MILESTONES NEVER MET

To those who hold unspoken dates
in their heart
milestones never met
I see you.

I see the movie that plays in your mind
of a future that never was
and yet
was
for you.

To those who ride the rollercoaster
of creating life
and losing life
before life even began
I see you.

I see the pain you buried deep
the empty place
you will never fill
for fear of forgetting.

To those who hold unspoken dates
in their head
milestones never met
I see you.

CHRISTMAS DAY

The lights won't chase the darkness
you left behind
but I put them up and try
anyway
the present I'm unwrapping
won't make me smile
knowing you're not here
on Christmas Day

The songs we sang together
won't bring you near
for they're not sung in the way
you used to do
there's a world so very full
of Yuletide cheer
but that world is not the same
without you

There's a log in the fire
burning merrily along
but the wine in my hand
has no taste
there's a tree twinkling fiercely
with such festive joy
but I fear all this joy
will go to waste

There's a space at my table
that's set for you
there's a joke you always told
which waits in vain
there's a hole in my heart
which never seems to mend
but nonetheless when I toast
I'll toast your name.

LOVE ME STILL

If you wish to love me still
when I leave
you can
by loving others
by giving new love
by not losing hope
by still seeing joy
by living your life
like it cries to be lived
by letting go
when the natural order demands it
by being at peace
with the circle of time.

If you wish to love me still
when I leave
you can
by loving life
by loving all that is life
by loving yourself most of all
the way that I loved you.

For now that I cannot
you must.

Love yourself
and you will love me still.
Love your life
and you will love me still.

MOTHER'S DAY WITHOUT HER

For many
Mother's Day is one
to be avoided
one to dread
to *rage* at.

But consider this
if you have a mother in heaven
who you miss so much
that this day burns like fire
then you have been blessed.

So many do not know this love.
So many
do not understand a love
so deeply bonding
that the grief
is beyond comprehension.

And consider this also
if your mother is no longer with you
on this mortal coil
do not
for a moment
believe her to be gone
that you are *without* her

for that is not possible.

She beats
with your every heartbeat.
She breathes
with your every gasp.
She is coded
into your every cell.

That cannot be undone.

Perhaps, *perhaps*
you could begin to celebrate
on Mother's Day
and every day
that you were gifted a mother
like yours.

And instead of avoiding this day
perhaps
perhaps
you could embrace it again
and invite her to be with you
again.
Remembering
as you did on earth
how blessed you were.

Perhaps
perhaps
this day could become a sweet one
once more
as you do all the things you know she loved
on earth
for her.

For many
Mother's Day is one to be avoided
but I wonder if maybe that could change.

I wonder if she is waiting for that
perhaps she is waiting for that?

WITHOUT A CHILD

To the mothers without a child
on Mother's Day
or any day
my heart goes out to you.

To those who have lost
to those who never had.

To those for whom a scribbled card
would mean the world.

To those who dream of grubby hands
salty tears and sloppy kisses.

My heart is with you on Mother's Day
and every day.

To battle on without your mother in this world
is tough
but to battle on without your child
is a daily torture
that flows against
the grain of grief.

If this is you
you are a warrior my friend.
And I see you
and all that you endure.

AGAIN

We'll meet again of that I'm sure
and though I should not rush
I know that time is running out
I wish the clocks to hush

For there is more I need to do
that you would hold so dear
and then I've lots to tell to you
when once again we're near

I'll tell you of the starlit nights
and know you saw them too
looking from a different place
but seeing the same view

I'll make you laugh with tales of joy
adventures through and through
I'll dip my toes in crystal seas
and bring that back to you

We'll meet again of course we will
till then sweet time must bend
I have so much to do until
I see you once again.

THE LIVING

The living
wish the dead
peace
and the dead
wish the living that too

The living
wish the dead
no *pain*
and the dead
wish the living that too

The living
wish the dead
great *joy*
and the dead
wish the living that too

The living
wish the dead
alive again
and the dead
wish the living that too.

IF I EVER HAVE TO LEAVE

If I ever have to leave you love
please know I didn't choose it
you were my every waking thought
my world
I wouldn't lose it

If I ever have to leave you love
don't think I didn't fight it
if I had any choice at all
we would never
be divided

If I ever have to leave you love
I truly rue the day
I always thought I'd be with you
beside you
come what may

If I ever have to leave you love
please know I'm always there
that somehow I will find a way
to show you
how I care

If I ever have to leave you love
the one thing you must know
is that you meant the world to me
I didn't
want to go

If I ever have to leave you love
you'll always have my heart
never fear my soul is near
even when
apart

If I ever have to leave you love
try to hear my laughter
and see my smile once in a while
let me live with you
hereafter.

IF A STAR FELL

If a star fell from the sky
every time I thought of you
the world would be so dark
the night a deathly hue

If a leaf fell from a tree
every time I wished you near
the forest would be bare
a winter all the year

If a wave stopped crashing in
every time I saw your smile
the shore would be so bleak
a barren rocky pile

If a song was never sung
each time I ached for you
the land would be so quiet
pleasures would be few

But none of this is so
the world keeps turning round
and though you're gone from sight
by love we're always bound.

BEFORE AND AFTER

You may find that you begin
to measure your life
before
and after
they left.

And that's okay.

Just be sure
whatever you do
whatever tiny grain of strength
you have left
that you strive
to fill up the after
as richly
and as beautifully
as they helped you fill
the *before*.

The before
is committed to memory now
but the *after*
is totally up to you.

Make it count.

LAST NIGHT

Last night you came to see me
when the darkness had no light
you stepped into my room
and I felt your spirit bright

You told me you were happy
and removed of earthly pain
you said I must believe
that our paths would cross again

You told me you were proud
of the life I carry on
you said you're keeping close
that I'll never be alone

Last night you came to see me
and when morning came around
I knew I wasn't dreaming
by your feather on the ground.

GIANT

You were so giant in this life
my love.

As though you were the galaxy
and everyone else the stars.

You were so full
of life
in this life

that in death
you are the same
giant.

And the hole you have left
is giant too.

You were so giant in this life
that my grief for you
must be giant also

that's the science you see.

And really
there is little to be done
about that.

For love breeds grief
grief breeds love
and a giant hole
does not easily fill.

THE ORPHAN

For what are you
when your parents pass on
other than an orphan?

A child without parents
is a child indeed
regardless of how old
they may be
or how many children
they have themselves.

And it is okay
to lament your orphan status.

It is okay
to feel aggrieved
that you are without.

Just remember
that when you *had*
you were one of the most lucky in this life.

And that some orphans
do not know
what it is to have been that.

I've not learned to live without you

perhaps I never will?

the truth of the matter is

you are always with me still

MAYBE

Maybe people don't want
to stop grieving

maybe they are terrified
that the grief they feel
is the last thing they have left
of that person

that if they move on from the grief
they will lose the final connection
the only tie.

Maybe people feel united
with their loved one
in the realm just outside our reality

united in pain and loss
banished to a parallel universe
where they can both exist together
still together.

Maybe that's just too precious
to move on from.

So if you are in this place
or you know someone who is
perhaps you can remind them
that they are connected
to their lost one
in so many more wonderful ways
than just the loss.

How can they not be?

Inch for inch
the pain they feel
equals the love they shared.

At the end of the day
it's all just love
and there is no need to banish either.

They can exist side by side
grief and love.

And they do
every day.

I NEEDED YOU TODAY

I needed you so much
it hurt to breathe.

There's nothing I wouldn't give
to hold you
one more time
and tell you how much
you mean to me.

I hope I told you this enough
when you were here.

I hope you can hear me now
when I say it
inside my heart
over and over
and over.

I love you.

I wish you could see
what is going on
in this world
you left behind
can you see?

I can almost hear
your words of comfort
this too shall pass.

I needed you today.
I needed you so much
it hurt to open my eyes
and see a world
without you.

I can almost feel you beside me
are you beside me?

I like to think that's you
sitting with me
in the darkness
through the hard times.

Like you always did in life.

FOR THE PARENTS

For all the parents
who are out there
living, walking, eating
even laughing sometimes
yet feeling as though
they are hollow
on the inside

this is for you

Losing a child
is like losing your life
and yet you are still here
still breathing
still paying bills
still talking about the weather
still loving those left
but never feeling whole.

A life lived
in black and white
a life lived without fulfilment
for how can anything ever replace
the little hand you once held?

Even if the hand was fully grown
at last touch
the mark it leaves
is infant
newborn
precious
it cannot be replaced
an emptiness
forevermore.

If you know someone living
this life
be aware that it will never
stop hurting
it will never stop grasping the air
out of their lungs
in the middle of the night.

The grief will never end
it will remain
like a hole

love them hard
they need it more

than you can imagine.

BEAR WITH ME

Bear with me as I grieve
I am not home
I do not live
inside my bones

Bear with me as I grieve
I do not hear
I cannot see
through blinding tears

Bear with me as I grieve
I am not whole
I lost a part
of vital soul

Bear with me as I grieve
I am not home
I do not live
inside my bones.

a bittersweet truth

    that a beautiful life

        will leave much grief

    in its wake

ON THOSE DAYS

On those days
when you miss someone the most

as though your memories
are sharp enough
to slice through skin and bone

remember how they loved you.

Remember how they loved you
and do *that*
for yourself.

In their name
in *their* honour.
Love yourself
as they loved you.

They would like that.

On those days
when you miss someone the most
love yourself harder.

FOR THOSE LOST TO WAR

For those who have fallen
for those who will fall
for those not yet born
and won't be born at all

For those who have lost
a daughter or son
for those who must stay
and watch their world burn

For those who defend
for those sacrificed
for those who lay trembling
in bunkers at night

For those who have fled
to lands far away
for those who don't know
where they'll wake up each day

For those who have fallen
for those who will fall
for those not yet born
and won't be born at all.

A MOURNING MOTHER

Pray you never tell a mourning mother
that she may try again for another
for how can she take comfort
in the new
when she is stitched by love
to the *was*?

Pray you never tell a mourning mother
that she may be more lucky
next time
for the next time will not negate
the life
she will never see play out
except in bittersweet daydreams.

Pray you never suggest to a mourning mother
that loving another child
could somehow lessen
the loss of one.

Motherhood
is a mystical and wondrous thing
and we love the life that lives within us
fiercely and forever
so we will grieve for that long too.

Pray you tell a mourning mother
that you see her pain
that she is brave
and loving
and strong
and that she will carry her little love
with her forevermore

for that is how it is.

TRAGEDY

When you have lost someone
in a very tragic way
normal grieving rules may not apply.

You see, you are dealing with so much
too much
you are processing death
you are processing loss
you are processing a new world
without them in it

but you're also processing
the horror of their end
the sheer *trauma*
and trauma has a way of working itself
into muscle, bone, brain and blood.

If you feel your breath
impossible to catch sometimes
it is no wonder
you are in shock
and even when that shock dissipates
underneath it will be trauma.

So, if this is you
if you are in this world of pain my friend
please seek help
please be kind to yourself
please slow down your world
and centre your wellbeing
at the forefront of priorities.

You will need much time to heal.

YOU MAY BE GONE

You may be gone
but I feel you
when the cool breeze
brushes past

You may be gone
but I hear you
when the music
plays its last

You may be gone
but I know you
as a painter knows
their art

You may be gone
but I feel you
in the chambers of
my heart

You may be gone
but your laughter
is still my
favourite sound

You may be gone
but my darling
you're ever
all around.

LESS

You don't miss someone less
as time goes on
you miss them *more*
because quite simply
you've been without them
for longer.

Once you accept that
it becomes much easier
to find a way to miss them
with peace
with love
with approval
from yourself.

Even with a little lightness.

And perhaps
you learn to turn the pain
into a passion
a passion to live *for them*
without them.

You don't miss someone less
as time goes on
you miss them more

just in a different way.

IT'S IN THE KNOWING

It is in the knowing that you loved
hard
whilst you could
that your wounds will begin to heal.

It is in the knowing that your person
was not unloved
or rejected
or uncared for.

It is in the knowing
that if you could do anything
anything at all
to bring them back
you would

no question.

It is in the knowing of all of the above
that you can begin
to plaster the cracks in your heart.

Because you *loved* them
and that is all you could have done
and a soul that was so loved
will always be at peace.

I hope that one day
you can find some peace
for your soul too
because goodness only knows
you have endured too much already.

IF YOU MUST

Cry if you must
but laugh more
because laughter
was
our
thing

Weep if you must
but sing more
because
such joy
music
brings

Sleep if you must
but walk more
because in
those woods
I
roam

Grieve if you must
but live more
because you
are
not
alone.

YOUR FOOTPRINTS

May you rest now, in peace
your toil has reached its end
and a life like yours deserves
a restful glory

May you sleep now, at last
the slumber of the loved
you have lived each chapter of
your wondrous story

May you pass now, it's time
if permission speeds your way
we let go with love, for love
is what you gave

May you know now, in life
you were treasured every day
and we daily walk the paths
your footprints made.

WHEN YOU REST

I write down how
I would like to be laid to rest
and who I would like to own
my best possessions.

I write down lists
of what you need to know
even the music I wish to be played
as you say goodbye
to my body.

But what I cannot seem
to write down
is the love that roars
from my toes to my hair.

And how
as my fingers grace the keyboard
the pain pulsing through
is almost unbearable.

How
the very thought of
your grief
makes me want to live
even more than I already do.

And how I would rather die
a million times
than leave you
with sadness in your life.

I cannot seem to find
the words to explain
how it feels
to be dragged away

kicking and screaming
from those you love most.

But then somehow
from somewhere unknown
the peace comes in
the *acceptance*
the *understanding* of life
and its circle.

And once that acceptance
is within my grasp
the only thing left
is to wish that same for *you*.

It is my time
and it is not yours
and I want
very much
for you to find the peace
I have.

And then I will rest
when you rest

when you rest.

FEATHERS

I left you a little white feather
I placed it right there in your way
I wrapped it in love with a message
to let you know you'll be okay

I drew you a colourful rainbow
it followed your car for a while
I made a spectacular rainbow
I hoped it would show me your smile

I flew down a beautiful robin
it landed right there on your ledge
I prayed he would give you the strength
to push yourself back from the edge

I try every day to remind you
that I never did go away
the feathers, the rainbows, the robins
are my way of trying to stay.

ROOTS

When I said *always*
I meant it you see

there was little in life
could divide you and me

and even in death
there is scarce to be done

when the soul who departs
was so loved by someone

when I said *always*
I meant it you see

our love still as strong
as the roots of a tree.

THE LIFE YOU DIDN'T LIVE

It's the life you didn't live
that plays
like a movie in my mind

the places you didn't see
the people you didn't meet

It's the new home
you never bought
the new car
you did not drive

the holidays you didn't take
and the sea air
you did not breathe.

It's the laughs you did not have
and the friends you did not hug
the birthday candles
you didn't blow out
and the gifts
unwrapped.

It's the life you did not live
that plays like a movie in my mind

A movie I would give anything I own
to see take place

in real time.

GRANDMOTHER

A grandmother
is an unfiltered source
of unconditional love

so if you had that
like me
I am so very glad for you.

A grandmother
is often the teacher
of all things

the one who passes on her wisdom
her sayings
her lessons
and many of these we will take with us
all the way.

And often a grandmother
is the one who teaches us
grief

by leaving
first

a happening she prepared us for
but we still could not be ready.

SUNSHINE BARRED

I thought
of how I would feel
looking down on my loved ones
crying
doors locked
blinds down
sunshine barred.

I thought
of how I would feel
watching them make life small
enough to mirror
the way they feel inside
because I am gone.

I thought
of their pain
their misery
their precious days
ever running out
spent in grief for me.

I thought
of all this today
and I took a very deep breath
looked for you in the sky
my love
opened my blinds
unlocked my door
and stepped out into life.

I thought
I felt you smile
and breathe out
at last.

PEACE AT LAST

Every day I wonder
were you afraid
did you change your mind
did you immediately regret
when you left that day?

Every day I wonder
could I have done more
said something wise
to make you see
that there are other ways
to stop the pain?

Every day I wonder
if you are up there
looking down
seeing what you had
that you just couldn't
clear your vision to behold
when you were here?

If you are
I hope you have found
the *peace*
you so sought here on earth

the peace that outran you
at every turn
the peace that was never
within your reach.

Because you deserve that peace
my love
at long last.

And I will try to take peace from that.

I will try to take peace from that.

FATHER'S DAY WITHOUT HIM

If you listen very closely
you can hear the words he'd say
when once again the calendar
falls hard on Father's Day

Don't make a fuss around me
it's just a silly day
I don't need any gifts
or a card to help you say

But then he'd tear the wrapping
and a wholesome smile would bloom
knowing that he made the love
that fills this little room

So when that day comes round
and he's no longer in your reach
remember that you know the way
and now it's yours to teach

A father is a feeling
a chamber in your heart
so fill that chamber up
and let your brave new life re-start.

THE MIST

One day the mist is going to clear
and you will re-emerge from that fog
different
as though you left a part of you in it

because you did my friend
you did.

You left the part of you
that wanted to go with them
the part of you
that couldn't face a life
without them

you left that part there
in the mist
and that is exactly
as it must be.

Because you needed space
you see
space to carry
your loved one
with you
as part of *you now*.

And when you come out of that mist
it will take you some time
to see
the new version of you
missing one part
and housing another

but you will.

One day
the mist is going to clear
and you will re-emerge
from that fog
different
as though you left a part of you in it
and brought a new part of you out

because you did my friend
you did.

THERE WILL ALWAYS BE LOSS

There will always be loss
there will always be gain
there will always be sunshine
to dry up the rain

There will always be light
there will always be dark
there will always be damage
inside of your heart

There will always be joy
there will always be pain
there will always be ways
to remember their name

There will always be death
there will always be life
and that plain simple truth
will still cut like a knife

There will always be loss
there will always be gain
there will always be sunshine
to dry up the rain.

don't yearn for me

though out of sight

I'm in your heart

and holding tight

THAT MOMENT

There will often be much left unsaid
when someone leaves
and so will commence many days
of asking yourself
was I enough
did I do enough
did I love enough?

You will replay the final moments
and your heart will fear
that they felt pain
that they suffered too much
and that will haunt you in the night.

But I believe
with all my heart
that heaven rinses those souls
of their pain
their hard memories
their regrets
and their fear
washes all of that away
and leaves only peace.

And that heaven exists
in *that* moment
that *washing away*
that *deliverance of peace.*

There will be much unsaid
when someone leaves
but none of it will matter
because they will know
in that moment
they will know.

A LITTLE BIRD

A little bird told me
you're living the dream
content in the new world
you've found
free as a fledgling
emerged from the nest
flying so high above ground

A little bird told me
you found those you lost
and you're resting as loved as can be
that you just wouldn't hear
of me joining you *yet*
because love wants you *living*
you see

A little bird told me
you often come down
and lay your cool hand
on my head
reminding me I've still a life left to live
and it's not time
to be with you
yet.

AFTER A WHILE

After a while
the brain forgets some details
the ins and outs
the timelines.

And your battered heart
may panic a little
because you fear you are losing
the person you already lost
a little more.

But no
it's the *feelings*
you remember.

The way someone made you *feel*.

It's their smell
their sound
their *presence*.

You never
ever
forget the essence of a person.

It's as though
all that time
you were connecting
on a much deeper level
and that's what stays with you.

And that's what never leaves.

WAS ONCE LOVE

I could tell you to remember
that grief was once love
and that if you stare at it long enough
you will see that it is love *still*.

I could tell you that
and I know you would perhaps
find some comfort there
but maybe what you really need to hear
is that grief is *awful*
and it hurts

and regardless of the love it was born of
you would wish it away
every minute
of every day.

It's okay if you are not winning
the battle
over the pain
it is not your burden to fight it
every day
but you deserve to feel peace
again
and you deserve to be free
of the suffocating misery.

So, give today to the grief
but tomorrow
maybe
you can look for the love once more.

TAKE THEM WITH YOU

If someone you love
did not make it on that trip
you can take it
for them
with them.

If someone you love
did not witness that milestone
you can show them
anytime you like.

If someone you love
did not get to do *their* living
you can finish those dreams
on their *behalf*.

The beautiful thing about love
you see
is that death
need not stop **life**.

If you carry someone
in your heart
you can take them with you

anywhere you like.

ACKNOWLEDGEMENTS

Thank you for buying this book, or if someone has gifted it to you, remember each time you open the pages how very valued you are. I would love to see you on my social media accounts where we daily remind each other that grief is still love turned upside down and inside out.

'They can exist side by side
grief and love.

And they do
every day.'

If you have been affected by any of the topics raised in *Loss*, you may find it helpful to talk to your partner, a relative, friend or reach out to one of the services below. You do not have to be in a crisis to call, you might just need a listening ear or to find help for a friend in need.

Cruse
For anyone affected by grief, Cruse offer bereavement support and information, no matter how long someone has been grieving.
www.cruse.org.uk

Samaritans
Round the clock support for anyone who needs to talk.
www.samaritans.org

Mind
Dedicated to better mental health, Mind provides details of resources and support in your area.
www.mind.org.uk

Sands
Offering support for anyone who has been affected by the loss of a baby before, during or after birth.
www.sands.org.uk

The Good Grief Trust
The website offers hope and specific resources for every kind of loss, whether it be a parent, friend or from an unexpected event.
www.thegoodgrieftrust.org

SAMH
For support and information in Scotland, SAMH also offers free, safe and confidential access to qualified mental health professionals online.
www.samh.org.uk